IMPRESSIONS of
ENGLAND

Produced by AA Publishing

© Automobile Association Developments Limited 2006

Published by AA Publishing (a trading name of Automobile Association Developments Limited, whose registered office is Fanum House, Basing View, Basingstoke, Hampshire RG21 4EA; registered number 1878835)

ISBN-10: 0 7495 4859 2
ISBN-13: 978 0 7495 4859 9
A02804

Printed and bound in Thailand by Sirivatana Interprint Public Co Ltd

Front cover: Row of 18th century thatched cottages, Exton, Leicestershire

IMPRESSIONS of
ENGLAND

Picture Acknowledgements

All photographs are held in the Automobile Association's own photo library (AA World Travel Library) and were taken by the following photographers:

Adrian Baker 77; Peter Baker 22, 34, 51; Jeff Beazley 11, 92; Michael Busselle 87; Malc Birkitt 3, 20, 36, 85; Ian Burgum 57; Chris Coe 17; Steve Day 8, 23, 27, 29, 43, 58, 66, 69; Steve Gregory 86; Anthony Hopkins 12, 59; Richard Ireland 14, 25, 93, 95; Caroline Jones 26, 28, 52, 62; Max Jourdan 21, 37, 46, 70, 82; Cameron Lees 24, 68, 78; Tom Mackie 15, 16, 18, 38, 39, 44, 45, 53, 55, 56, 64, 74, 83, 88, 90, 94; Jenny McMillan 32; Eric Meacher 13; John Miller 65; Roger Moss 5, 50, 80; John Mottershaw 54; Hugh Palmer 35, 72, 91; Tony Souter 19; David Tarn 10, 73; Rupert Tenison 41, 76, 89; Martyn Trelawny 84; Andy Tryner 42; Wyn Voysey 7; Linda Whitman 30, 40, 47, 60, 71; Harry Williams 19, 49, 61; Peter Wilson 67, 79; Tim Woodcock 31, 81; Jonathan Welsh 63.

Opposite: Tehidy Woods, Cornwall.

INTRODUCTION

England is a small country, but it's packed with all manner of sights and scenery. Stick a pin on the map at random, and you're sure to find an area full of surprises. Chances are, within shouting distance there'll be swathes of beautiful, open countryside or magical forests and lakes; there'll be hidden corners of history, tranquil villages and ancient market towns; and there'll be magnificent stately homes, industrial monuments, gardens, outdoor museums – not to mention the cities, with their galleries, theatres, shops and restaurants.

At a pinch, you could drive from one end of England to the other in a day. Yet few countries can claim so visible a wealth of history and such variety of landscape over such a relatively small area – travel just a few miles and everything changes. *Impressions of England* celebrates this diversity and richness, its images capturing the best of this ancient land, the familiar and the unexpected, from venerable Stonehenge to the vibrant heart of London.

For every part of England has its own special appeal. The West Country has lush green hills, smugglers' bays and rocky sea-cliffs, with a clutch of glorious cathedral cities to contrast with its picturesque market towns and villages. In the southeast, London's breathless pace and world-famous landmarks are the main focus – but even the capital's broad commuter belt has its own rural havens in the Sussex Downs and the wonderful orchards of the Weald of Kent. To the west lie the delights of the hidden corners of Hampshire, along with its historic ports, the New Forest and the holiday resorts of the Isle of Wight. The Cotswolds have a distinctive charm, based on the golden stone of its buildings.

For a unique and evocative experience, roam the low marshlands and enjoy the wide skies and abundant birdlife of the East Anglian fens. The great industrial cities of the Midlands and the North – Birmingham, Manchester, Leeds and Newcastle – have reinvented themselves as hotbeds of culture and nightlife; and then there are the plunging valleys, open moors and isolated farms of Yorkshire to discover; the glowering peaks of Derbyshire; and Northumberland's rolling hills, border fortresses and empty, majestic coast. The natural beauties of the Lake District, in the northwest corner of England, draw millions of visitors each summer to admire the drama of the narrow passes, soaring mountains, plunging waterfalls and serene lakes of this outstanding scenic area.

Whatever tickles your tastes as you explore England's diversities and curiosities, this wonderful collection of photographs will provide the perfect appetiser.

Golden Hill, in the Dorset town of Shaftesbury.

*Rievaulx Abbey, set in the valley of the River Rye in Yorkshire, was built in the 13th century by monks
as the Mother Church of the Cistercian Order.
Opposite: classical columns decorate the houses in the Palladian-style Circus in Bath, built by
John Wood the Elder in 1754.*

Wharfedale is the longest of the Yorkshire Dales, with meadows and drystone walls bisected by the parallel paths of Wharfedale Road and the River Wharfe.

Looking towards Housesteads Crags along Hadrian's Wall, which stretched about
73 miles (117km) from Bowness, on the Solway in the east, to Wallsend, on the Tyne in the west.

The gritstone escarpment in Staffordshire known as the Roaches, which marks the southwestern edge of the Peak District. At the far end is the outcrop called Hen Cloud.

Stonehenge, the mystical stone circle on Salisbury Plain in Wiltshire.

Mupe Bay on the spectacular stretch of coast near Lulworth in Dorset. The shingle beach can only be reached by boat or foot, and much of it is inaccessible due to landslides.

Buttermere in the Lake District. There are two further lakes in the Buttermere Valley:
Crummock Water and Loweswater.

Ashness Bridge in the Lake District, with Skiddaw Mountain in the background.
Opposite: the chalk cliffs known as the Seven Sisters, East Sussex.

The fossil-rich white and red chalk cliffs at Hunstanton, Norfolk.

Ponies have roamed the heaths and woodland of the New Forest for centuries.

The lighthouse at the end of Portland Bill, in Dorset, guides boats through the hazardous waters between the Bill and the Shambles sandbank, a stretch known as the Portland Race.
Opposite: punting past Clare College on the River Cam, Cambridge.

Beaulieu Palace House, in Hampshire, was formerly the 14th-century great gatehouse of Beaulieu Abbey.
The house, which has been in the Montagu family since 1538, has a famous vintage car museum.
Opposite: the fan-vaulted ceilings of Gloucester Cathedral's cloisters date back to the 14th century.

Marsden Rock on the northeast coast of Tyne and Wear, home to thousands of sea birds.

Statue of George Loveless, leader of the Tolpuddle Martyrs. The six farm labourers formed the first trade union in their Dorset village in 1834, for which they were prosecuted and transported to Australia for seven years.

The harbour at Lyme Regis, Dorset, with Golden Cap hill behind.
Opposite: oak trees at Westonbirt Arboretum, in Gloucestershire.

A medieval castle and church crown St Michael's Mount, the rocky island off the south coast of Cornwall.

Isambard Kindom Brunel's SS 'Great Britain', in Bristol Docks. She was launched in 1843 to provide luxury travel to New York.

Looking towards Malham Cove, a curved inland cliff of carboniferous limestone in North Yorkshire.

Warkworth Castle, built on a hill in a loop of the River Coquet in Northumberland. The Percy family acquired it in the 15th century, but it fell into ruin when they chose nearby Alnwick as their principal residence.

*London's Houses of Parliament, otherwise known as the Palace of Westminster,
and the famous clock tower housing the huge bell, 'Big Ben'.*

Swinsty Reservoir in the Washburn Valley, North Yorkshire. It was constructed in 1876 to provide water for Leeds and Bradford.

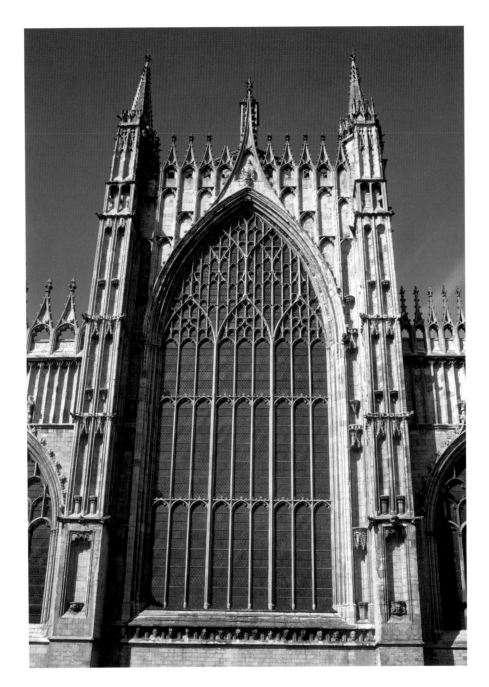

The east window of York Minster, the largest Gothic church in England.

View of Arlington Row, a row of weavers' cottages in Bibury, in Gloucestershire. They were converted from a monastic wool store in the 14th century.

The River Great Ouse near Littleport Bridge, in the fenlands of Cambridgeshire.

Mute swans at Abbotsbury's Swannery, on the shore of the lagoon enclosed by Chesil Bank in Dorset.

View of Ullswater from Hallin Fell; the lake is the second largest in the Lake District.
Opposite: beach huts at Wells-next-the-Sea, on the north Norfolk coast. The town, although now about a mile
inland, is still a working port.

Hardy black-faced sheep graze the frosty flanks of Swaledale, in the Yorkshire Dales.

The ruined engine houses of Botallack Mine on the Cornish coast: shafts extended under the sea.

The church in the grounds of Ilam Hall, Staffordshire. Like the mansion (now a youth hostel belonging to the National Trust), it was rebuilt in the 19th century.

The Clifton Suspension Bridge spanning the Avon Gorge, Bristol. Brunel was just 24 when his design for the bridge won the competition to find an engineer for the project.

Fields of lavender are grown commercially at Heacham, in Norfolk.
Opposite: Scafell Pike in the Lake District – England's highest mountain at 978m (3,208ft).

Durdle Door, the sea-cut rock arch on the spectacular stretch of the Dorset coast near Lulworth.

Inside the great choir of Rievaulx Abbey, North Yorkshire. In its heyday, about 150 monks and 500 lay brethren lived and worked at the abbey.

St Mary's Lighthouse and its adjoining buildings stand on a small island – accessible at low tide – north of Whitley Bay, Tyne and Wear.

Bolam Lake Country Park, Northumberland, is famous for its birdlife, and particularly for its resident mute swans.

The Cheesewring, a granite pillar on Bodmin Moor, Cornwall. It was formed by natural erosion, though legend claims it was created as the result of a competition between the Saints and the Giants of the area.

The Mausoleum and New River Bridge on the huge estate of Castle Howard, north of York.

The White Horse at Westbury, one of seven such figures carved into the chalk downs of Wiltshire: this is the oldest, dating back about 300 years.

Holkham Bay, north Norfolk. It forms part of a national nature reserve comprising sand dunes, saltings, marshes, pasture and woodland.

The harbour at Scarborough, Yorkshire's prime resort. Castle Headland separates the two sandy bays.

Tranquil Derwent Water, in the Lake District National Park.

The Hall House on the main square of Lavenham in Suffolk, originally built in the 1390s.

Golden Valley, named after the River Dore, on the Herefordshire / Welsh border.

Bamburgh Castle, still a private home but open to visitors, in Northumberland.
Opposite: the Cotswold Way, a long-distance footpath, at Painswick Beacon, Gloucestershire.

Durham Cathedral's Chapel of the Nine Altars, with its beautiful rose window.

Clavell's Folly, or Kimmeridge Tower, above Kimmeridge Bay in Dorset. It was built as a summerhouse in the 1820s by the Reverend John Richards, who inherited the surrounding Smedmore estate in 1817.

The lighthouse at Lizard Point in Cornwall, which marks the most southerly point of mainland Britain.

Oak and beech woodland on Alderley Edge, a dramatic red sandstone escarpment on the Cheshire Plain.

Municipal deck chairs at Eastbourne in East Sussex, one of the south's premier seaside resorts,
with a 5-km (3-mile) promenade.
Opposite: mirror reflections on the water at Buttermere, in the western Lake District.

A series of 'outdoor rooms' characterise the Arts and Crafts garden at Hidcote Manor, Gloucestershire.

Yorkshire's Bempton Cliffs – one of the best places in England to watch sea birds.

Antony Gormley's landmark 'Angel of the North', on a hilltop above Gateshead. Made of steel and standing 65ft (20m) high, it has wings almost as long as those of a Jumbo jet.

Cheddar Gorge in the Somerset Mendips: Britain's highest inland limestone cliffs, riddled with spectacular caves.

The coast at Robin Hood's Bay, a onetime fishing and smuggling village south of Whitby, in Yorkshire.
Opposite: Tower Bridge, an iconic London landmark since 1894. The central span is split into two equal
bascules, or leaves, which can be raised to allow river traffic to pass.

The old warehouses at Gloucester Docks have been transformed into a vibrant area of museums, specialist shops, restaurants, bars and cafés.

One of the curiously shaped formations known as Brimham Rocks in the Nidderdale area of the Yorkshire
Dales. Inevitably, many of the boulders – eroded millstone grit – have been given fanciful names.

Castlerigg Stone Circle, near Keswick in the Lake District, is thought to be one of the earliest in Britain, dating from about 3000 BC. It is believed to have had astronomical significance.

The ruins Fountains Abbey, near Ripon in Yorkshire. It was founded in 1132 by 13 Benedictine monks, who broke away from the abbey in York to follow the stricter Cistercian Order.

Part of the Studley Royal Gardens, landscaped around the ruins of Fountains Abbey (see page 75).
Opposite: catching waves at Newquay, on the north coast of Cornwall: Fistral beach is one of the
best in the country for windsurfing.

The tomb of Grace Darling in St Aidan's churchyard, Bamburgh. Grace became a local heroine when she rowed out with her father to save the crew of the 'Forfarshire', which had struck the rocks.

The narrow promontory of Spurn Head, at the mouth of the Humber Estuary. The lighthouse became redundant in 1985.

The Calstock Viaduct was built in 1908 to carry the branch line from Plymouth to Gunnislake over the River Tamar, which forms the county boundary between Cornwall and Devon.

Alnwick Castle, home of the Duke and Duchess of Northumberland, has belonged to the Percy family since 1309. It had been a border stronghold since the 11th century and a town grew up beside it.

Ruined Corfe Castle in the area of Dorset known as the Isle of Purbeck. An important royal castle in medieval times, Parliamentarians destroyed it in the mid-1600s.

Opposite: Little Langdale, a scattered hamlet in the Lake District valley of the same name.

Gritstone boulders on the moors above Todmorden, near the border of Yorkshire and Lancashire. The unfenced moorland has been used since the Bronze Age, and commoners retain the right to graze their livestock there.

Dover Castle, facing the English Channel on the Kent coast, has been of major importance in defending the country from Europe for nearly 2,000 years. A maze of tunnels is dug into the cliffs.

Appleton-le-Moors, on the North York Moors, is a good example of a single-street village with traditional houses, parallel back lanes and a common.

The South Downs near the village of Alfriston, East Sussex. A national trail follows the range of chalk hills for about 100 miles (160km) between Eastbourne and Winchester, in Hampshire.

Hardknott Roman Fort, dramatically sited near the summit of Cumbria's isolated Hardknott Pass.

St Ives, the perfect Cornish village: sandy beaches, a rocky headland, cobbled streets, a harbour...

During migration and in winter, the sandflats and saltmarshes of Morecambe Bay in Lancashire are important feeding grounds for thousands of wading birds and wildfowl.

The heart of the Cotswolds: pastoral beauty near Withington, southeast of Cheltenham, in Gloucestershire.

The River Allen, near Hexham in Northumberland.

The detached chalk stacks near Swanage in Dorset known as Old Harry Rocks – possibly because the Devil used to lie down on the cliffs here.

The Langdale Pikes (Pike of Stickle, Loft Crag and Harrison Stickle) tower over the Great Langdale Valley in the Lake District.

Pollarded willows by King's Sedgemoor Drain, an artificial drainage channel on the Somerset Levels.

INDEX